Here is a **LIFESIZE** *Allosaurus* footprint.
Put your foot on top and see whose is
the biggest! *Allosaurus* could run around
34 miles per hour, which makes it
one of the fastest dinosaurs **EVER**.

First American Edition 2019
Kane Miller, A Division of EDC Publishing

First published in Great Britain 2019 by Red Shed,
an imprint of Egmont UK Limited.
Text and illustrations copyright © Sophy Henn 2019
Consultancy by Professor Mike Benton.

Library of Congress Control Number: 2018952952
Printed in China

LIFESIZE

Sophy Henn

DINOSAURS

and Prehistoric Creatures

Kane Miller

A DIVISION OF EDC PUBLISHING

Dinosaurs roamed this planet a long, long, looooong time ago (between 252-66 million years ago, in fact), so sadly we can't go to a zoo to see them. That makes it tricky to picture just how big a *T. rex's* smile was . . .

Tricky, but not impossible! Every time you see the word **LIFESIZE** in this book, you will know you are looking at a dinosaur or part of a dinosaur that is actual size.

So come on! Let's go on a **LIFESIZE** adventure and see how you measure up against some of the smallest and **LARGEST** dinosaurs and prehistoric creatures.

This is a **LIFESIZE** *Microraptor* – one of the smallest dinosaurs we know of. Although he had wings, he couldn't fly! Instead he would glide from tree to tree looking for a tasty lizard to eat. YUM!

Let's start at the very beginning . . .
dinosaurs began their lives as eggs!
And those eggs came in different shapes,
sizes and colors, just like these **LIFESIZE**
dinosaur eggs . . .

WOW! This **LIFESIZE**
Beibeilong egg is the largest
known dinosaur egg **EVER**.

This **LIFESIZE** *Deinonychus*
egg is hatching – awwwww,
how cute! But not for long,
as this little dino grew up
into a deadly predator!

Quite possibly the smallest dinosaur
egg is this **LIFESIZE** *Massospondylus* egg.
But *Massospondylus* wasn't the smallest
dinosaur ever – see how big it grew
at the back of this book!

This **LIFESIZE** *Diplodocus* egg would have been laid in the forest and then covered with earth and leaves. Once the baby hatched, it would push up through the earth and have to fend for itself right away.

Here is a **LIFESIZE** *Maiasaura* egg – the baby dino inside was around 12 inches long and curled up into a tight ball to fit inside the egg.

OUCH! This **LIFESIZE** *Utahraptor* claw looks super sharp. Hold your foot up to the page and see how it would look on you!

Utahraptors had a claw on each foot that curled up at a sharp angle so it didn't touch the ground when they walked along. This kept it super sharp for hunting, which was something raptors were really, really, **REALLY** good at.

Can you believe that among these deadly dinosaurs, millions of years ago, bees were buzzing about? The oldest bee found, trapped in amber, was .1 inches long and 100 million years old!

Gastonia had some of the best body
armor of all the dinosaurs. It also had
a spikey tail that came in very handy
for fighting off predators, like these
Utahraptors . . . watch out!

You are nose to **LIFESIZE** nose with a *Diplodocus*.
Can you flare your nostrils as big as his?

Diplodocus was one of the longest dinosaurs EVER. It had a **REALLY** long tail that it could whip at supersonic speeds, which made a **VERY** loud **BOOM**. It made this noise to scare away predators or to show off to other _Diplodocus_.

To be this completely GINORMOUS, _Diplodocus_ had to eat A LOT. In fact, it had to eat so much that it didn't even have time to chew, so _Diplodocus_ just gulped down its food instead.

Being so HUGE meant *Diplodocus* didn't
have to worry too much about predators,
but *Allosaurus*, with its super hunting skills,
was thought to have been its biggest threat.

How does this **LIFESIZE** *Stegosaurus* plate look on your back?

Imagine having 20 more, like an actual *Stegosaurus!*

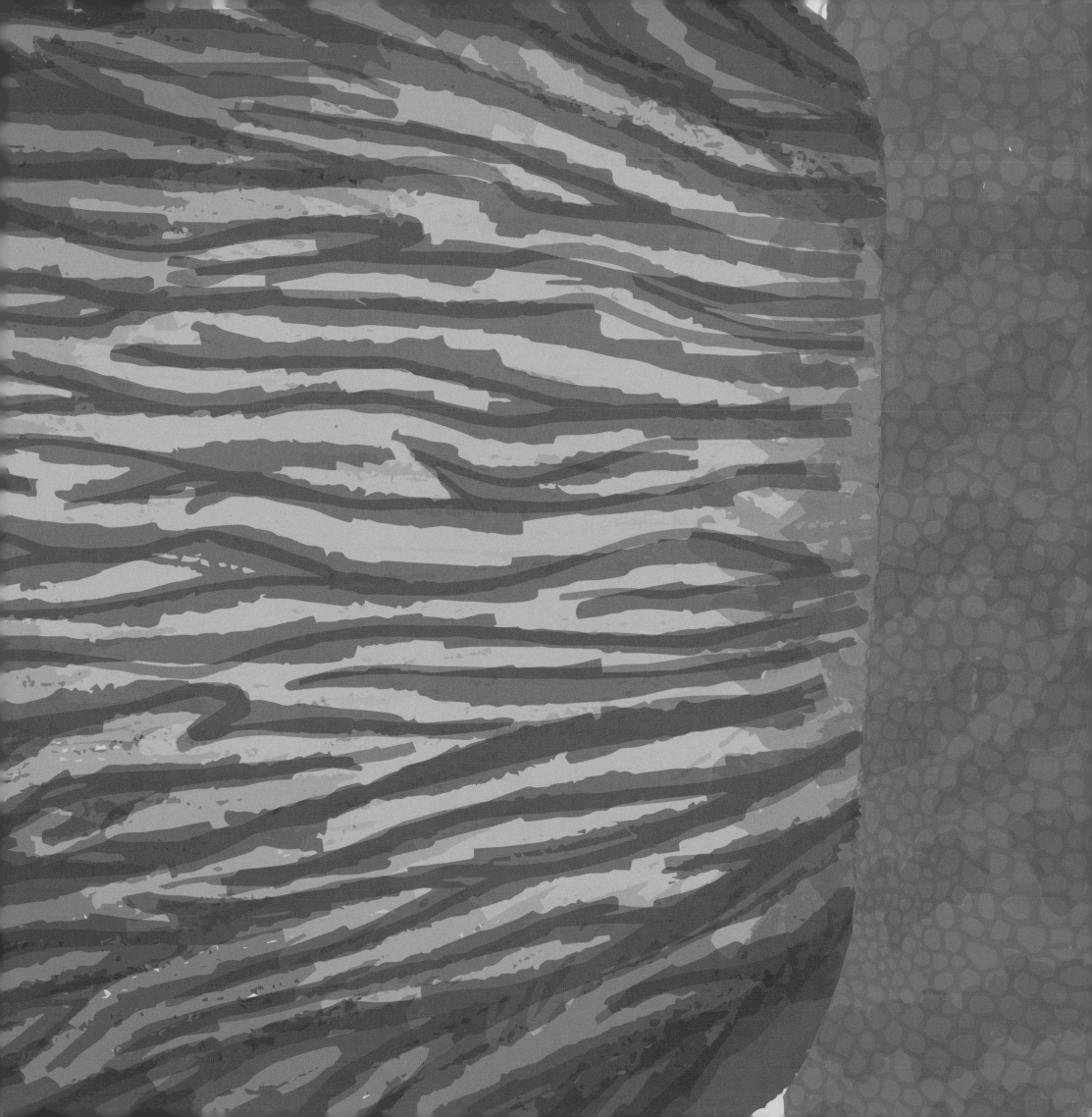

Stegosaurus was actually quite a snazzy dinosaur. It could change the color of its back plates when it was competing for a mate or for territory.

Although it looked fancy, *Stegosaurus* wasn't so clever. Its brain was only as big as a walnut.

Allosaurus was probably *Stegosaurus'* least favorite dinosaur. It had a habit of eating them! *Allosaurus* was a fearsome hunter with 70 serrated teeth and a really big mouth – all the better for biting with!

Isn't this **LIFESIZE** *Pteranodon* beak HUGE?
Hold it up to the side of your nose and
see how it looks on you!

Pteranodon were not dinosaurs or birds, they were actually flying reptiles. They didn't have feathers but had wings made of stretched skin that they used for swooping and soaring.

Pteranodon would soar above the sea looking for fish, diving down to catch them in its beak.

This long-necked creature is an *Albertonectes*.
It was a plesiosaur, which isn't a dinosaur but a marine
reptile. With such a long neck (about 23 feet!), the
Albertonectes could only swim very slowly and flapped
its flippers a bit like bird wings to propel itself forward.

Say cheese! See how your toothy
grin compares to this **LIFESIZE**
Tyrannosaurus rex's sneaky smile!

Tyrannosaurus rex might have been the most powerful land predator to have ever lived, and had the biggest teeth of all the dinosaurs ever, but it couldn't stick its tongue out! *T. rex's* tongue was attached to the bottom of its mouth, so it couldn't blow raspberries either!

Triceratops means "three-horned face." Its fancy neck frill was made of solid bone and most likely used for showing off to other *Triceratops*.

Although it was a favorite meal of *T. rex*, *Triceratops* was a plant eater and had around 800 tiny teeth for cutting up leaves.

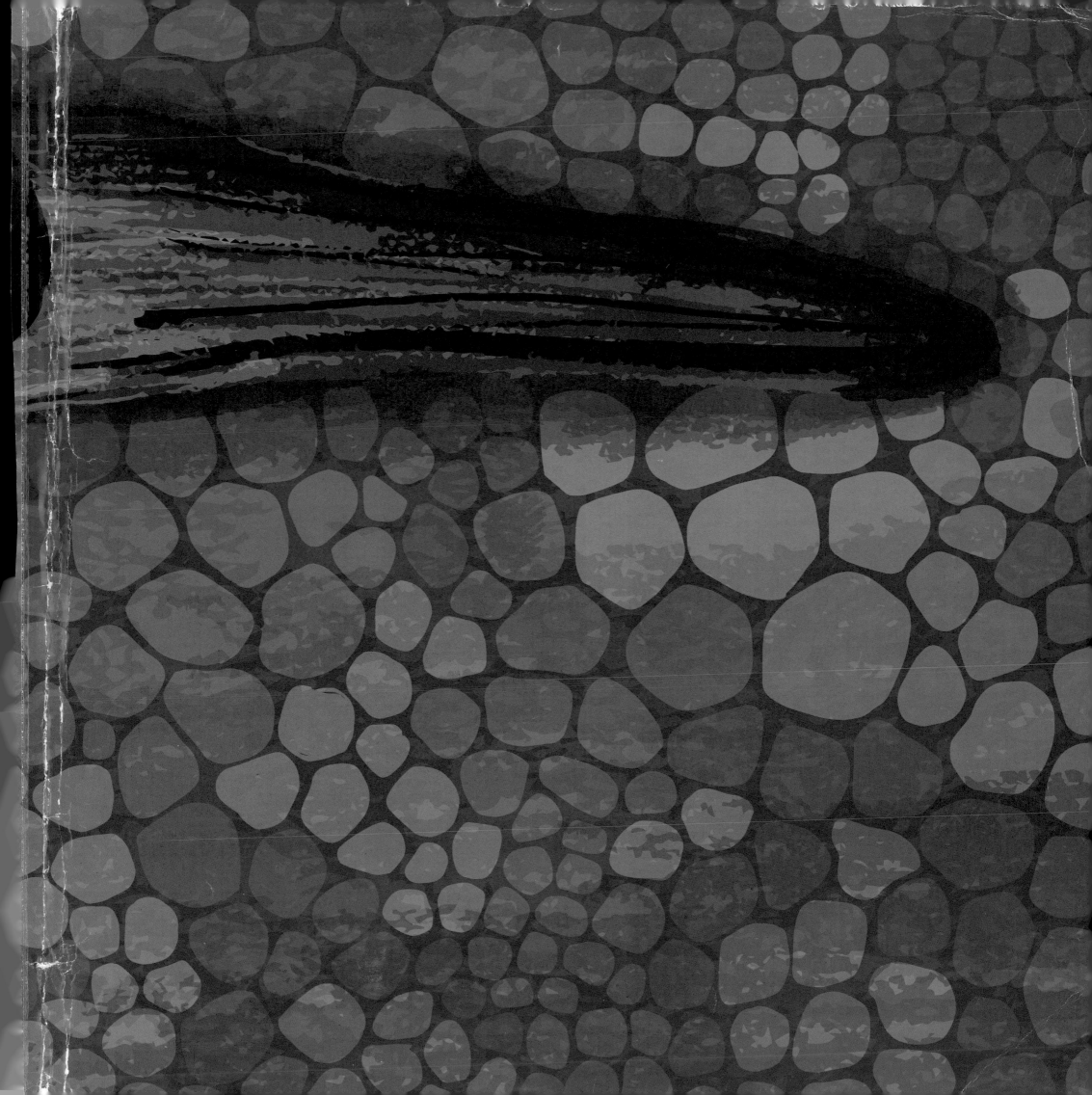

Wow! We've traveled back in time to see some amazing **LIFESIZE** dinosaurs and prehistoric creatures. Let's see how they compare in size to one another. And then measure yourself using the book to find out how you compare.

Pteranodon (TEH-ran-oh-don)

Wingspan: around 19.5 feet

Did you know? *Pteranodon* had a beautiful head crest that kept its head balanced and helped it steer when flying.

Diplodocus (dip-LOD-er-cus)

Head to tail: around 82 feet

Did you know? Throughout its whole life, *Diplodocus* never stopped growing!

83 LIFESIZE books

Allosaurus (al-oh-SORE-us)

Head to tail: around 28 feet

Did you know? An *Allosaurus'* head was so big and heavy that if it hadn't had such a big tail it would have just fallen over!

Stegosaurus (steg-oh-SORE-us)

Head to tail: around 29.5 feet

Did you know? *Stegosaurus* means "roof lizard."

30 LIFESIZE books

28 LIFESIZE books

Beibeilong (BAY-bay-long)

Head to tail: around 26 feet

Did you know? *Beibeilong* is the largest known feathered creature to have lived! And a good reminder that birds are actually living dinosaurs!

27 LIFESIZE books

Maiasaura (my-ah-SORE-ah)

Head to tail: around 29.5 feet

Did you know? *Maiasaura* began life walking on two legs but walked on four when it got older.

30 LIFESIZE books

Tyrannosaurus rex (tie-RAN-oh-SORE-us rex)

Head to tail: around 29.5 feet

Did you know? *T. rex* had a REALLY big mouth and could eat around 500 pounds of meat (about half a horse) in one BIG BITE!

30 LIFESIZE books

Massospondylus (mass-oh-SPON-di-luss)

Head to tail: around 13 feet

Did you know? Massospondylus had five fingers and a thumb-like digit on its hands.

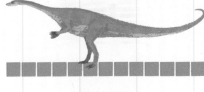

13 LIFESIZE books

Utahraptor (YOU-tah-WRAP-tore)

Head to tail: around 19.6 feet

Did you know? *Utahraptor* had the largest brain for its size of any known dinosaur, so it might have been the smartest!

20 LIFESIZE books

Deinonychus (DIE-non-i-kus)

Head to tail: around 10 feet

Did you know? It's from studying these dinos that we now know birds are descended from dinosaurs.

10 LIFESIZE books

Microraptor (MIKE-ro-RAP-tor)

Head to tail: around 2.6 feet

Did you know? Microraptor means "small thief."

3 LIFESIZE books